On the

On the Way Home

REFLECTIONS FOR OLD AGE

---

*Edited by Frances Makower
and Joan Faber*

Illustrations by Margaret Tournour

*Introduction by
Elizabeth Longford*

DARTON · LONGMAN + TODD

First published in 1994 by
Darton, Longman and Todd Ltd
1 Spencer Court
140–142 Wandsworth High Street
London SW18 4JJ

ISBN 0-232-52062-3

A catalogue record for this book
is available from the British Library

Typography by Humphrey Stone
Phototypeset by Intype, London
Printed and bound in Great Britain
at the University Press, Cambridge

Contents

Introduction

I warmly welcome this inspirational anthology on old age; there are not enough of such books, although old age has always seemed to me a perfect subject for written reflection. In old age we have the maximum number of experiences to draw upon, the time is ripe for self-assessment and we can rely on God to end the proceedings if they begin to pall.

I find this series of reflections most appealing; some are almost awesome and all come straight from the heart. I am also particularly enchanted with the frequent touches of wit and humour. Every one of these frail or failing members of the Society of the Sacred Heart, speaking her mind on old age, is still able to look at the world with wonder, even vitality.

One of the contributors, Arati Snow, has now died at the age of eighty-five, but in her lovely poem, 'Foreshadowing', she confessed that she found the beauty of children, art and music as captivating as ever. How, she asks, can she – and the rest of us 'oldies' – learn to live in two worlds at once, as we must do during the last years, unless God sends us physical reminders?

Window frames warp, the floor cracks,
And weariness and rheumatism have their hour.

Without these reminders, how would we ever 'look up and away' to God?

The joint editors of this collection, Joan Faber and Frances Makower, have added a brief quotation from the Bible after each piece, followed by a pertinent question or two addressed to the reader. Thus after presenting us with Arati's 'Foreshadowing' they lightheartedly ask, 'Is your semi-detached still desirable?' As an 'oldie' myself, I answer with a wholehearted 'Yes' and I thank Arati for helping us to see the ills of old age as a 'preparation for the rehabilitation of the resurrection' rather than simply the delapidation of the 'semi'.

I must also stress again the good humour and serenity of these twenty-one contributors and their skilful editors. Even the pieces we might expect to indicate sadness and regret turn out to be preludes to hope. Lydia Collado's 'Heart in Winter' is not 'frozen' but 'feels', 'risks', 'waits'; Patricia Mackle's 'Dry Sticks' form crisscrosses on the ground to symbolise the resurrection of Christ; old age brings a vision to Margaret Williams which she describes in 'On Mount Tabor'.

I wish I had the space to pay tribute to *all* of these reflections, each one with its own special excellence: the touching story of the old man's bowl, the old women dancing, the potential of old age and the claims of both dependence and independence to be seen as spiritual gifts. The opening piece, 'Journey Home' by Rebecca Ogilvie Forbes, holds pride of place for me. Not only was the writer ninety-eight when she wrote it, but she unveils in simple language the glorious paradox of 'Home': '. . . not a much loved place, but a Person . . . Love itself and for ever.' How could we, she asks, do otherwise than celebrate old age? Perhaps this piece provides a reply to the old nun we meet in another contribution. She is longing, above all, to meet her mother in heaven, and Joan Faber relates how she asks anxiously, 'But do you think she will recognise me?'

Finally a word on the structure of this anthology. Poetry and prose are equally balanced. All the contributors, except one, are old; they were born between 1895 and 1959 and their average age is seventy-five. All of them have been, or are, teachers of some kind; many combined teaching with administration, medicine, psychiatry, the arts or writing. Eleven different nationalities are represented, and there are many references to working with the poor.

Years ago I read a story in a newspaper about a group of millionaires who were planning to escape death by having their bodies stored in a deepfreeze to be 'revived' at a future date. This anthology shows that there is only one way to live for ever: not in a deepfreeze but in high heaven. And the road there is not lined with refrigerated boxes, but with the achievements of old age.

ELIZABETH LONGFORD

Journey Home

Events and impressions of long ago are often more vivid in old age than are more recent ones. To me, the memory of arriving home for the holidays is one of these, and my heart still senses its thrill.

It was at the end of a long train journey – fourteen hours in those days, followed by several miles' travelling into the country – that the climax came. As we neared the house through the woods, we came to a large wellingtonia which, standing at a corner where three drives converged, successfully blocked the view; as we rounded the tree the sense of anticipation was almost more than I could bear, then, suddenly it seemed, *home* was there!

In memory it was not so much the people awaiting us that drew me it was just the fact of *home* where every stick and stone was known and loved. This thrill was repeated twice a year for a decade, and now, some eighty-five years later, the memory of it is as vivid as ever.

Is this a picture of life? It is such to me: a long journey, not to be measured by hours or days but already comprising the greater part of a century, with the most tremendous of arrivals at its end.

The nearer that moment, the greater the anticipation as the climax approaches. As before, the goal is at times partially obscured: pain, the various strippings of age, the dimming of eyesight and hearing and memory, the losing of loved ones who have beaten us to heaven – these may at times lessen the view. But there will come at last the great moment when we round the last obstacle

and there – here – is *home* ... not a much loved place,
but a Person ... Love itself and for ever.

How could we do otherwise than celebrate old age?

REBECCA OGILVIE FORBES

'Leave your country, your kindred and your father's house
for a country I will show you.' GENESIS 12:1

Have you been called upon to make long journeys?

Did you travel alone? In the dark?

Which star or stars guided you?

Keep in Mind

In the opening scene of *Hamlet* we are confronted by darkness and shouting as the guards cry out in confusion, 'Who is there?' That search and cry reverberates in an unresolved way throughout the play. Reflecting on the time I spent at Duchesne House, where we care for our frail and elderly sisters, I am left with this same question: 'Who is there?' Was I speaking to someone fragile and diminished, or to a vibrant, active person, or was I comforting a frightened, dependent child? Probably all of these, all the various personae that we have each lived throughout our life, but, that being so, to whom did I speak? How do we recognise and move from one persona to the other, without either confusion, or loss of respect and infinite love for the frail, old person before us?

I like to think that our development is circular rather than linear and that 'in the end is our beginning'. At the end we have once more the need to find someone who can hold us in mind, even as our mother held us as infants. For it is the mother's awareness of her baby which keeps her infant ever present, constantly in her mind, wherever she or her baby is at any one moment. The mother holds, contains in her mind, and then mediates and hands back all the various and complex feelings of both her baby and herself; feelings which are now safe, since they have already been handled and accepted. The infant needs to be 'held in mind' to avoid the experience of disintegration, or that of annihilation.

I feel that those who are close to the very old need to have this sort of reverie in order to hold or contain some of the fears which may feel childish, both to the old person and to those caring for her. Such a reverie will ensure connectedness, even when the old person is caught in the chaos of senility. Mothers and infants do not have, nor need, a verbal communication, but both know instinctively of anxiety, fear and the desire for closeness. So at the end of life, with increasing needs that spell out dependence, we should be able to offer safe holding and containing and 'keeping in mind'. We cannot allow ourselves to misconnect, for that will make old people feel as though they have lost a part of themselves.

But 'Who is there?' As we look at the mentally alert, physically fragile old person, with our memories of them in their heyday, when they were models for us and were themselves people of significance, we are taken aback to find them passive and waiting; they may even be in touch with the child's fear of not being recognised by a mother after a separation. Once I asked a frail old sister, 'Who are you most looking forward to seeing when you get to heaven?' 'My mother', she replied, 'but do you think she will recognise me?' Her mother had died leaving a forlorn little three-year-old.

Being with the very old, we face reality, nothing is hidden or masked, certainly not death. We are confronted by mystery, the mystery of Christ in his death and resurrection. This has led me to reflect on the mystery of silence. The Lord himself experienced this both at the beginning and end of his life. 'While all things were in quiet silence, thine almighty Word leapt down from his throne' (Wisdom 18:14). No words could express his passion, his call to live his exodus and return to the Father. He, like us, had to tread the passage from birth into adult life, and then break through to total abundance of life. For him and for us, this is silent mystery. For those in this final stage of transition, the Word which has nurtured during life can still be received in deepest silence, the Word can still reach through to the very marrow of being. We see a sister who is senile, but who can still find her way into the chapel, sit there in rapt contemplation before, with shining eyes, she receives the host; this she holds in her hands, bending over in silent adoration. Truly, right to the end, there is an inner and consuming fire of love.

Our three most precious gifts are life, love and time. In this holy and humble period of waiting for the moment of final ecstasy, these gifts are still present. We, who silently stand and watch in awe, must contain and keep in mind these gifts, so that we may give them back; we must validate them, thereby enabling them to be lived without anxiety and in the secret truth of each person's life. We know so little of the final purification and preparation for our true life. There is at this time longing, disappointment, anxiety, with the wearisome waiting, depression, and questioning about how God is present or absent. Again, so much of this has to be intuited, held in mind, for much of it seems to defy words, as though a pre-verbal experience has taken over once more. Once someone who had been known for her very simple and direct prayer appeared to become depressed; in fact she was anxious. She feared that she had displeased the one who was her very life, for he was silent and absent. This fear needed to be put into words and it was old and favourite quotations about the mercy of the Pierced Heart of Jesus that brought her stillness.

As in all families, each person is different and unique, so we who are allowed to be near to those in their final life/death experience need to pray for the gift of reverie, so that everyone, in whatever guise they come to us, may be silently 'held in mind'.

JOAN FABER

Do not be afraid, I am with you ... I give you strength, truly I help you, I hold you firm with my saving right hand. ISAIAH 41:10

Do you feel the need to be held?

Do you have someone to turn to?

Are there people whom you are attempting to hold?

Where do you find your strength?

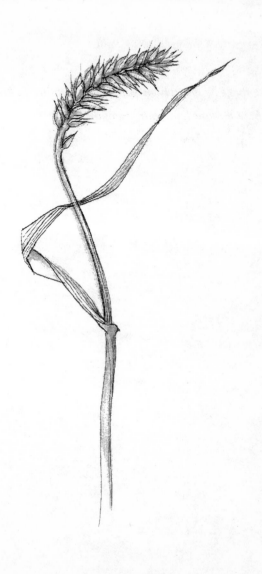

Golden Slippers

I used to take the stairs
Two at a time,
Running up the stairs,
Or even sometimes
Down.
Running, running, running.

Now I sedately step
Into an elevator,
Riding down and down
And up and up,
Smooth and slow,
Smooth and slow.

Soon,
With quantum leap to light,
I'll fly on wings of wind
On and on and on –
And I'll wear golden slippers
When I walk the shores.

CARMEN SMITH

They will come shouting for joy on the heights of Zion
... The young girl will then take pleasure in the dance,
and young men and old alike. JEREMIAH 31:12, 13

Do you long for, or do you dread, the final journey?

Can you put your feelings into words – for yourself or for others?

Are you actively aware of friends in heaven?

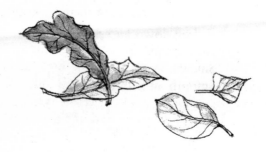

Old Age Observed

Last year as I was recovering from hepatitis I was sent to Poitiers. There I found several communities of our retired sisters. Everyone in my small group was active, but we shared common life with the other frailer communities. We joined together for both the liturgy of the Mass and for more informal times of prayer; we took our meals together and frequently met as we talked, watched television and shared our memories and dreams.

I found much to admire in these older sisters. Together they created an atmosphere of prayer in which the beauty of the Mass and the Office were the high point of our days. The liturgy was so well prepared; music was carefully chosen to replace weak voices. I was inspired by the charity of the whole group and by the way they cared for each other. They visited the sick among themselves, read to those who could not see and made sure that anyone in a wheelchair had a place of honour around the altar for Mass.

I was also impressed by the dynamism of the various communities. Not all are handicapped and many are very busy. One ninety-year-old looks after the library, another sees to the flowers and decorations for the chapel, someone else sells small articles for the missions and yet another provides for the intellectual stimulus of the communities, arranging talks, films, discussions, etc. Some also undertake activities outside. They visit lonely old people, take children for catechetics, keep up a considerable correspondence and one, an eighty-year-old, belongs to the group who keep the cathedral clean and takes her turn with a broom.

I enjoyed living in this atmosphere which conveys, so movingly, the essential of our lives. Many of these sisters had been outstanding in their day; among them were former mistresses of studies and headmistresses. Now they are called to live out our charism of Charity. They can do no more, but dare any of us do less?

BRIGITTE TRIBOT LASPIÈRE

'I was hungry and you gave me food, I was thirsty and you gave me drink, I was a stranger and you made me welcome, lacking clothes and you clothed me, sick and you visited me, in prison and you came to see me.'
MATTHEW 25:35–6

What do you receive from neighbours?

What do you give?

Would you be missed if you suddenly moved from your neighbourhood?

What has moved you in your observation of old age?

What Would Be

Not what I see, but what God sees *in me* –
Past, present, future with capacity ...
Bifocal, three-dimensional, four-square,
Full faceted – naught hidden can impair
God's vision. Well may confidence believe
That our goodwill may *everything* achieve,
For who but God – while knowing what *could be*
Will yet bestow his love on what *would be*!

My gleaming goal, then, God – our wills so fused
That no potential of mine unused
May hinder that high plan of what *could be*
But love's desire accomplish what *would be*!
   So help me, God!

DOROTHY BLOUNT

I keep Yahweh before me always,
for with him at my right hand, nothing can shake me.
So my heart rejoices, my soul delights,
my body too will rest secure.
PSALM 16:8–9

Are you content with what has been or do you yearn for
what might be?

Do you have a friend with whom you can share your
dreams?

What blocks your dreams?

The Wooden Bowl

Fifty-eight years ago, as a child of twelve, I read a story in a book that was in use in my Belgian school. I imagine that it was a simplified version of an old French folktale. Whatever its origin it made an indelible impression on me: I was for the first time deeply affected by 'literature', and by the sheer truth and power of the 'moral' of the tale. The pain and pathos of the story still tug at my heart.

Once upon a time a little boy lived with his parents, poor peasants, in a simple hut in the woods. The parents loved their child, and he returned their love and was a good son to them, young as he was.

Also living with this family was the grandfather of the little boy. He was old and frail and no longer able to work. He sat all day in his chair, and when he came to table he was so shaky that he could hardly eat, and made a great deal of mess around his place. One day his trembling hand caused him to drop and break his platter and spill all the food on the ground.

The boy's mother was furious. She shouted at the poor old man, shook him and said that henceforth he would eat all his meals from a wooden bowl as he was not fit to eat from a plate like normal people.

Ashamed and humiliated, the old man withdrew from the table to a corner, where, isolated and lonely, he ate only from a wooden bowl like a baby.

One day his parents noticed the little boy busy with a knife and a block of wood. 'What are you doing? What are you making?' they asked.

'I'm making bowls for you both to eat out of, when you are old', he answered in his simplicity.

At this his parents were shocked into a realisation of what they had done. They burst into tears, embraced the old man and drew him back into the family circle, where he lived out his days, cherished and honoured.

APRIL O'LEARY

For wisdom opened the mouths of the dumb and made eloquent the tongues of babes. WISDOM 10:20

Where do you seek wisdom?

Do you receive insights from unexpected places?

Have you ever been surprised to discover that your words, quite often long forgotten, have brought comfort and wisdom to another?

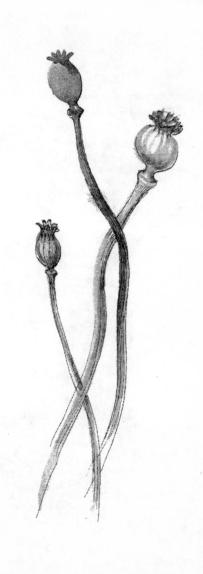

The Heart in Winter

The heart in winter feels
  sensitive to lifeless,
  if not hopeless, self.

The heart in winter mourns,
  cries for painful loss.
  Deep hurts, experienced
  and buried, surface
  the spring when it was not allowed to bloom;
  the summer when it was not allowed to play;
  the autumn when it was goaded to let go.

The winter heart rests tranquil,
  accepts the truth of being,
  reflecting and praying
  on all that matters,
  learning to compassionate itself
  and all who never learned to be.

The heart in winter hopes,
  gathering strength, yearning for rebirth,
  searching for lost and scattered dreams,
  finding sense in labours wasted.

The heart in winter risks;
  breaks ice in freezing cold,
  opens doors on hidden joys,
  casts shadow upon darkened rooms;
  with faded hues blends colour.

The heart in winter waits,
    watching night move into day,
    to bring to light God's greatest gift:
    the seed of love
    that refused
    to die.

LYDIA M COLLADO

In prayer we come to him with everything that touches
our life, with the sufferings and hopes of humanity.
CONSTITUTIONS OF THE SOCIETY OF THE SACRED HEART 1982

Do you mourn for loss?

What brings you comfort?

Treasure

Archaeologists attach great importance to the discovery of antiquities. Reflecting on this and on the current interest in television programmes like *The Antiques Roadshow*, it has occurred to me that we – the elderly – can discover similar treasures in our own lives. Life has been a great adventure ... things that seemed of little worth have been shown to have great value, just as uranium, once considered a waste product, has been found to be a source of atomic energy.

Coming to terms with ourselves on the eve of our dissolution, we discover with surprise the riches we have accumulated throughout our lives. Working, like the best tapestry makers, from behind – a stitch here, a knot there, using the colours God has given us – and when we turn it over

... a miracle! One day we shall see the result and will marvel at what God has done in us and through us.

We must never lose heart; our latent energy is greater than we realise: having suffered we have learnt patience; knowing our weakness, we can think more kindly of others; being used to discomfort, we can handle inconvenience. The wonder of each new day makes us optimistic and we expect the best: someone will smile at us, or repeat what we have not been able to hear; someone will give a helping hand on the stairs, or say something kind.

We delight in it all on awakening, thank God and try to do the same for others. At the end of the day, let us not ask whether we have been made happy, but rather, what have we done to make others happy today?

PALMIRA DE OROVIO
TR. JOYCE BLACKWELL

'The kingdom of Heaven is like treasure hidden in a field which someone has found; he hides it again, goes off in his joy, sells everything he owns and buys the field.'
MATTHEW 13:44

Have you found your field of buried treasure yet?

What are you prepared to give to purchase it?

Are you still finding treasure?

Are you aware of your accumulated riches?

Old Women Dancing

And so we danced.

Sandtracks through the whitened bush
lead riverwards
away from home . . .

Beyond the river,
the dry river,
our little cone-shaped 'Mountain of the Heart'
stood framed against the flaming evening sky
by black acacias,
ancient and beautiful.

Soon the stars will hang within our reach
and the half-seen kraal-encircled village disappear. . .

We reached the river-bed,
river of hard sand, ribbed and eddying,
cutting its curved way westward.

Down the high banks
the thorn-tree roots were bared
plunging to the unseen water
far beneath our feet.

Our river . . .
wild in the rare rains
but now a place of meeting.

And there we danced.

We danced because we met
other old women –

happy, hungry, drunk old women,
carrying their beer pots from their brewing,
from their drinking,
home to the village.

But we were empty-handed,
knowing no hunger, our hands were empty –
our white faces turned away from home,
offering nothing
except . . .
RESPONSE   RESPONSE   RESPONSE

Response to laughter and to greeting –
our empty hands outstretched
as we embraced
there on the dry river-bed
at sunset.

And there we danced.

Old women with old women
leaping and laughing and singing.

Night was near
And now we too were drunk –
drunk with the kinship of our years,
the shared pain and beauty of our womanhood.

For we, old women,
we were trees
rooted in the high dry river banks,
reaching for unseen water that the earth might live –
but trees that leaped and laughed together,
our branches tangling with the stars
even as the sun went down.

We were trees –
no longer limited by place,

twisted by time,
burdened by need.

We leapt and laughed and shouted and embraced –
lifted to touch the stars –
lifted beyond the stars –

For those short moments unafraid of night.

Because
we danced
together.

PRUE WILSON

They shall dance in praise of his name, play to him on
tambourines and harp! PSALM 149:3

What makes you want to dance?

Do you find people prepared to dance with you?

Have you time to dance?

Final Fiat

The church resounds to the echoes of the great Amen as hundreds of voices cry out their 'so be it' to the God who gave them life and voice. The myriad small amens of every prayer are caught in the desire that God be truly glorified by all creation, through the Word who gave it being.

And what of that other great Amen which lifts us out of this world, as we have known it, into the embrace of a loving and compassionate Creator? This last triumphant Amen becomes a celebration of all that has been, and a welcome to the new life opening before us. This 'so be it' finds an echo in every corner of our being as it catches up the countless amens of our past and offers them to the glory of God. It heralds the moment when at last we can surrender the final bonds that hold us tied to mortal existence and can surrender the life we have been given into the hands of the one who gave it. We endure this final disengagement from our world only to enter into a new and far deeper relationship. Amen to life as it has been; Amen to death as it opens a vast new horizon before us.

For most of us it is no easy thing to face death in peaceful surrender. The writer of Ecclesiastes tells us that there is a time to give birth and a time to die. How shall I meet the moment of death when it comes? The inevitability of dying is the one thing of which we are absolutely sure. Yet when the message of its approach comes, we can be taken unawares and we may be deaf to the message.

To deny the summons, to refuse to admit the unwelcome news is a natural expression of our reluctance to face this 'sacrament of separation'. Only when shattered equilibrium is rebalanced and our senses reordered can the inevitable be faced and death be recognised for what it is.

And for each of us this is a uniquely personal experience. For me, my death is unshared and unrehearsed. I will meet it as I have met the many little dyings of life's journey. The small amens of life will be caught up into this one great acclamation. My death is truly mine alone. No one can die it with me or for me. I must bear its weight alone.

But do I stand alone? Or do I stand before my God in Christ Jesus, the Word who took upon himself the burden of humanity, the pain of loneliness and loss, no less than of joy. The Word became mortal and in taking flesh learnt to stand with his creation in its growing, its flowering, and, above all, in its dying. Dying was not an easy passage for Jesus. He who could drink the dregs knows what this chalice holds for each of us. He is with us as we too face, in our own way, what for him caused drops of blood to soak the ground on which he lay.

It is no easy task to die, but we are not alone. The One who supported and held us through the many little deaths of life, will not leave us now. He has carried us through the surrendering of youth with its exuberant hopes, its idealism and promise; helped us through the loss of dear ones; has borne with us the diminishment of powers, senses, movement, even space, as we passed through the corridors of time to the restricted confines of a bed. Can we imagine that he will not be there at the very centre of our final dying?

I will surely be flooded with a confusion of feelings as my time comes to say goodbye to a world which has been the home of all my aspirations, faltering efforts, failures and achievements. This world which I have come to love is about to fall apart: a world of friends now to be left behind, of dreams yet unfulfilled, of hopes not realised and tasks still incomplete.

With so much yet to be done, even if poorly done, there will be regrets, anxiety, remorse. A welling up of nameless fears, confused emotions, surging anger, helplessness, a sense of isolation and aloneness. I may be impatient with those who try to help, alienated from those most close, or I may cling to them as I experience a numbness too deep to share, a vulnerability too painful to express.

The patient, unwavering loyalty and understanding of those close to us will bring comfort through this maelstrom of emotion. They will help us hold on in trust through the struggle as we look once more, with tears, at the tapestry of life. As we gather together the threads, we know that the true pattern is visible only to the Original Designer, the Great Repairer of all that has gone awry in the warp or woof of our lives.

And because we know that we are loved eternally and unconditionally and that others watch and pray with us, we will be able to look back at the full picture of our life, accept it as it has been, and turn forward to face the full reality of death with peace and dignity.

MARY D'APICE

'Can you drink the cup that I shall drink?' MARK 10:39

Are you aware of undergoing 'little deaths'?

How have you coped?

What do you fear most?

What do you long for?

Prayer for Latter Days

I want to grow old
comfortably,
life hanging on my shoulders
like an old sweater –
warm and loose
And shapeless.

Let my days and nights
move slowly
taking my shape,
old shoes –
looking like me
even when
I'm not wearing them.

I have loved life,
all of it,
an old friend –
faithful
to the very end.

Make me ready, Lord
to slip off
shoes and sweater
When my spirit
puts on eternal youth.

CARMEN SMITH

He emptied himself, taking the form of a slave, becoming as human beings are ... PHILIPPIANS 2:6

What have you observed of the detachments demanded of old age?

Would this be something you welcome or resist?

Can you find any advantages to this latter period of life?

Called

One childhood memory of my father remains in my mind. I was just four years old and was sitting comfortably on his knee, when he took a plum from the plate one of my older sisters was holding, skinned it and fed me with it. Two weeks later he died in England of meningitis. Thus our mother and we seven children were abruptly deprived of a loving and gifted husband and father. In later years I heard my mother say that she had had no time for a breakdown since all her energy was absorbed by moving from the country to a smaller house in Dublin.

It was in our new home shortly after we arrived that, standing alone in the garden and feeling estranged as I watched the October clouds float by, the desire formed in my mind. 'I want something that will never change', I thought. I suppose this was the first awakening to my need for God. Weak health necessitated a governess for a time, but I spent one summer term in our school at Mount Anville where I made my First Communion.

The first call to follow Christ came between the ages of thirteen and fourteen, but I had not the courage to speak of it to anyone. I left school at eighteen and enjoyed many years of diversion among places, people, jobs and entertainments. From time to time a small voice whispered, 'Where is this leading to?' And 'naught else contents thee that content'st not me'! But it was many years later while running the Barat Club in Hoxton, a very poor area in the suburbs of London, which I greatly enjoyed, that a convincing call came. Awakening one

night, I experienced heart and mind beating with the words, 'You have not chosen me, but I have chosen you.' At that moment I knew the game was up and silently said 'Yes' to God.

Catherine of Siena wrote, 'all the way to Heaven is Heaven . . .', but in no way was my journey along those lines. Entering the noviceship was incredibly hard as 'my harness, piece by piece, He hewed from me'. However, with the passing of time I realised that my gloom was after all but the shade of his hand outstretched caressingly. Now, in the evening of life, with harbour lights beckoning, I pray and give thanks for all I have received in and through our Society of the Sacred Heart.

CLARE SHANLEY

Everyone whom the Father gives me will come to me.
JOHN 6:37

Do you remember your first intimation of God?

Have you ever felt impelled by the Spirit of God to make a specific decision or to follow a particular course of action?

How did you/do you react?

The Ageing Tree

In the beginning
In the first garden
There stood a tree,
New, young, and beautiful,
Golden in the dawn.

Beneath the tree
Abraham entertained the angels
Shaded from the burning heat
Of noon-day sun.

One afternoon –
Dark with pain,
The tree stood
Stark and bare,
While thunder rent wide open
Every grave.

Now, aged and bowed
The tree with knotted, furrowed bark
And open side
Yet bears leaf and life,
Its roots down deep
In dark heart of the earth,
As, whitened by the moon,
It reaches for the stars.

And yet, unknown, unseen
The tree awaits the mystery divine,
Majestic – beautiful
Before the very throne of God.

MARGARET TOURNOUR

... one of the soldiers pierced his side with a lance.
JOHN 19:34

Have you ever been pierced? Has it happened often?

Where was God (for you) at the time? Did your opinion change with hindsight?

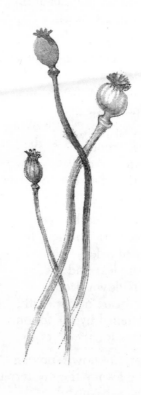

Aged conviction

'Sans teeth, sans eyes, sans taste. . .', wrote William Shakespeare of old age – and, I might add, sans legs! Is this a true description of what it means to be old? I think not. The weight of experience cannot be discounted: it gives depth and balance, even if forgetfulness sometimes disturbs.

To my mind the secret for contentment in old age is first of all to make, and re-make, a conscious act of surrender, letting go with cheerfulness and thanking for the abilities and activities now diminished or withdrawn. Secondly, to adopt a forward looking attitude: hopeful, expectant; after all we stand at the gate of Heaven, and surely it will open soon. Thirdly, and of primary importance, to strive to live the words of the Constitutions of the Society of the Sacred Heart: 'In prayer we discover that the fidelity of God dwells at the very core of our weakness.'

BARBARA HOGG

'My grace is enough for you: for power is at full stretch in weakness.' 2 CORINTHIANS 12:9

What helps you to overcome the weakness and dependence of old age?

What advice would you give to would-be carers?

Later Truth

Life has become History
and the imprint it has left
has marked it so that
nothing now can change.
Time has broken chains
and loosened shackles;
serene, in friendly waters
my boat now floats at rest.

What matter, if before me
there is no ground to walk on;
Living is a challenge,
an ever new excitement.
Faith sustaining ever –
knowing that at our side
Invincible Love is there
open to our love.

Although my footsteps falter,
I want to go on walking,
with or without felt support,
to reach the only goal.
The milestones on the route
guiding my ascent.
Open arms sustain me
when I falter.

I have longed for many things
and dreamed dreams,
in the light of later Truth
these seem but vanities.
The radiance of yesterday
that seemed transparent then,
diminished now –
opaque . . . no longer clear.

Tho' I live in shadows now,
alone among my ruins
there is a certainty in me
that nothing can destroy.
I hear a song of glory,
a cry of victory
and arms raised up, inviting
and calling me to come.

I see Him not, yet love Him
and hear the voice that thrills
behind the veil, perceiving
the outstretched, open arms.
O Beauty beyond splendour,
that face to face I'll meet
I know the hidden glory
of what awaits me there.

PALMIRA DE OROVIO
TR. JOYCE BLACKWELL

But at once Jesus called out to them saying 'Courage! It's me. Don't be afraid.' It was Peter who answered. 'Lord,' he said, 'if it is you, tell me to come to you across the water.' MATTHEW 14:27–8

Have there been occasions when it felt as if there was no ground beneath your feet?

What kept you going?

Have you any mental 'picture' of heaven?

How have you formed this?

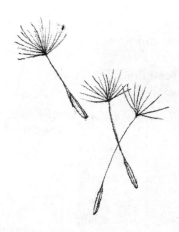

Foreshadowing

Long before the end, Lord,
You have given us so many hints,
Hidden invitations, snatched glimpses,
Of what lies beyond us, so that already,
The unknown life seems like home
And we learn to live in the two worlds at once.

As if to assure us that life there
Is indeed worth having.
How slowly, yet surely, you loosen our roots,
One by one, and we become aware,
That this semi-detached desirable dwelling,
In which we have lived so long,
No longer keeps out the wind and weather.
It seems that the roof leaks above our heads,
Window frames warp, the floor cracks,
And weariness and rheumatism have their hour.

I see all this, my God,
As your kindness, a gift from you,
A preparation for the rehabilitation
Of the resurrection.
For dawn still brings in each day with glory
Of wonder. The play of light and shade,
The splash of the river, the flash of a scarlet leaf,
Still enthrall.

Children are as compelling in their beauty,
Art, music, insights as captivating as before.
How then, without your reminders – the leaking roof,
The cracked floor, the warped wood,
Should I ever look up and away to you?

My Beginning,

My End

My Love,

My All in All.

ARATI SNOW

'In the evening you say "It will be fine; there's a red sky",
and in the morning, "Stormy weather today; the sky is
red and overcast. . ." ' MATTHEW 16:2–3

*Can you read the signs of the times – are you aware of the
Lord's hints?*

Is your semi-detached still desirable?

Potential

The winds came; rain and sun and substances in soil,
produced the tree that God has planned.

Chisel and hammer on marble block shaped the Pietà,
conceived in the mind of Michelangelo.

The aged woman was, potentially, within the newborn
child.

In old age there is a stillness which may allow the Holy
Spirit greater freedom.
It is a period similar to the cocoon stage.
Life is planned; it is no coincidence.
According to response, the human being grows into the
true image
in the mind of God.

And the good Lord has needed many, many years to
show me the breadth
and length, the height and depth of Heart.
And still more years to make me understand his
Kingdom,
as I have striven to become a royal subject.

Old age resembles trees, the consequence of buffeting
winds,
soothing, life-giving rain and warmth of sun.
Yet I have been more directly shaped,
shaped by choice and grace, at every moment
of my life.

THERESA MARY AGIUS

I went down to the potter's house; and there he was, working at the wheel. But the vessel he was making came out wrong ... So he began again and shaped it into another vessel as he thought fit. JEREMIAH 18:3-4

Are you aware of moments or periods when your life has been shaped?

What played the major part in those changes: people, events, love, gifts?

Magnificat Moments

As I come to the end of my sabbatical year I am in a celebration mode. It has been a magnificat year and God has poured into it hours and days I'll hold in memory. It has been a year filled with new relationships that grew and ripened in unexpected faith experiences.

After fifty years of religious life, I have returned to live in the novitiate (which I've learned to call 'the house of initial formation'). It has been a time of happy renewal – a second 'first' year of commitment and community. All the freshness and enthusiasm of first beginning in the Society has touched the steadiness and comfortable ease of a life lived and given, lived and given during these fifty years. In quiet celebration of our vocation – knowing again that God chose first – I have delighted to watch the initial formation of today's young women and to share their prayer. Through contact with their sensitivity for the suffering of the poor, I have become more aware of the real meaning of concern for the marginalised – the lonely, the sick, the abused, the hungry.

Somehow living with these younger women has made me more able to grow into old age without fear, without regrets, without resistance. I'd thought that when I was older it would be a time to pass on to the young what I've known and loved in the Society. In many ways I've found the young pass on to me their vision of the world and its need, their hope for the future and their dreams of how hope and faith can acquire 'a local habitation and a name'. So our treasures become not hand-me-downs, but hand-me-ups.

In her beautiful little book entitled simply *Old Age*, Helen Mary Luke uses King Lear's beautiful lines to point out what she considers are the proper occupations of old age: 'And *pray*, and *sing*, and *tell old tales*, and *laugh* at gilded butterflies.' *Prayer* – the attention of the mind and heart; *telling of old tales* – passing on the wisdom of the elders; *laughter* – the lighthearted delight in beauty and the pregnancy of the present moment; and *singing* – the lilting response of listening. In these later years, there is time for the steady response of magnificat to all that life has brought of joy and pain, darkness and light, springtime and winter of the spirit. This is the time to quietly, gently absorb the mystery of life, and to capture wonder.

So at the end of a year that has indeed been a Sabbath, I remember the mercies of the Lord, ancient as the stars and new with every dawn.

CARMEN SMITH

The Almighty has done great things for me. Holy is his name, and his faithful love extends age after age to those who fear him. LUKE 1:49

What marvels has the Lord done for you? How, and with whom, do you share them?

Do your paths cross those of young people? If they do, what do you give and what do you receive?

Dry Sticks

Leaves losing freshness turn to brown, crimson and
   gold,
   With trunks no longer taut and upright, bark
   roughened;
Boughs twisted, entwined, become grotesque.
Winds tossing meet less resistance, sap runs dry,
Branches fall and lie
Crisscross upon the ground in perpendiculars and
   horizontals –
   From these dry sticks are crucifixes made.

Classrooms now remote, ideas no longer sought.
   Students have scattered, dispersed around the globe.
Professional excellence has ceased to be a goal,
Opinions rest ignored.
With passing years, the carver seeking hidden riches,
Finds delicate graining, polished by time's passage.
Ideas crisscross.
From uprights and horizontals deep thoughts arise.
Life's boughs and branches meet and through
this welter of success, failure, acceptance and rebuff
   Are crucifixes formed.

Green or mature life.
   Both can form a cross,
On both can Christ be placed,
   From both come resurrection.

PATRICIA MACKLE

'When you were young you put on your own belt and walked where you liked; but when you grow old you will stretch out your hands, and somebody else will put a belt round you and take you where you would rather not go.'
JOHN 21:18

What gifts has old age brought?

Have these gifts surprised you?

Are you still making discoveries?

On Mount Tabor

Old age, for this old lady at least, has proved to be Mount Tabor. It has taken ninety years for us, the Lord and I, to climb this far, but now we are sitting down at last, by ourselves, very near the top. The view is glorious, a whole lifetime of the Lord's goodness, seen in perspective. We have come to this high place to pray together; the world is sorely in need of prayer.

And now he is showing me something of what he really is; he has become transfigured before me. He is wearing his earthly garments, but they are shining with unearthly whiteness. His face is radiant; his eyes are fixed on me as though I mattered. He is speaking to his Father who, unseen in a bright cloud, calls him 'beloved Son'. Is the bright cloud the Holy Spirit? Life has become trinitarian of late.

Two friends have suddenly joined us: Madeleine Sophie and Philippine. That shows that heaven is not very far away. He tells me not to be afraid, and touches me. It is good to be here, but he will not let me pitch a tent. We must wait under the stars for a time, until he tells us to stand up and set off for the last short climb to the door of home. It has begun to open.

MARGARET WILLIAMS

'Rabbi . . . it is wonderful for us to be here, so let us make three shelters . . .' MARK 9:5

Do you have a favourite prayer place?

What enhances your peace? What disturbs it?

Postscript – About the Sacred Heart Sisters

In the chaos of the revolutionary Paris of 1800, Madeleine Sophie Barat founded the Society of the Sacred Heart. Attracted to the contemplative life of Carmel, she was persuaded that the needs around her demanded a return to the knowledge of God's love and that this could best be effected through the influence of educated women. The Society and its schools, both for wealthy and poor children expanded rapidly in Europe and beyond. Schools were always the principal means of making known the love of the heart of Christ, but from the beginning Sacred Heart sisters ran orphanages, worked with seculars and organised retreats.

Today, the sisters number approximately 4500 and work in forty-one countries. In common with many religious orders, vocations in North America and Western Europe are scant, but in some areas, notably Uganda, the Philippines and Hungary, they are burgeoning. Moreover, changes following the Second Vatican Council have brought increased team work with secular colleagues and a broader interpretation of education. Formal primary, secondary and tertiary education remains a fundamental means of revealing God's love but today many sisters work in prisons, hospitals, AIDS clinics and advice centres. They work with the elderly, with youth groups, and are to be found among disadvantaged and marginalised people, for in the words of their Constitutions of 1982: 'The pierced heart of Jesus opens our being to the depths of God and to the anguish of humankind.'

In common with many religious groups, the charism

of the sisters of the Society of the Sacred Heart has been strongly influenced by Ignatian spirituality; whatever their work, their lives are rooted in prayer. They are called to be contemplatives in action.

FRANCES MAKOWER

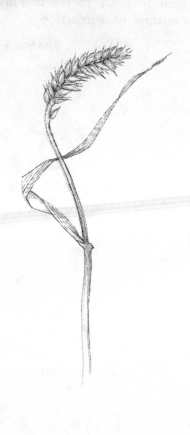

Notes on Contributors

THERESA MARY AGIUS (1915–   ) Professed 1955 Maltese

Theresa Mary spent her active religious life in primary and secondary education, serving as headmistress for over twenty years. For the last fourteen years she has been serving a parish and living in a small community.

MARY D'APICE (1922–   ) Professed 1954 Australian

Mary trained as a doctor and is currently involved in psychotherapy, spiritual direction and retreat work. She has also been involved in secondary and tertiary education and served as the principal of the Catholic Women's College of Sydney and Queensland.

JOYCE BLACKWELL (1912–   ) Professed 1943 Irish

As a teenager Joyce spent several years in Spain; she has been involved in education for most of her active religious life. From 1974–8 she went to the Society of the Sacred Heart's province of Venezuela, where she taught Spanish to illiterate poor children and English to children from wealthy families. Since her retirement she has worked for the peace movement, first in London with Pax Christi and now in Portsmouth with the Peace council of south-East Hampshire and the Integrity of Creation Ecumenical Group.

DOROTHY BLOUNT (1907–   ) Professed 1950 English

As a young adult, Dorothy looked after her parents; she therefore entered the Society 'late'. Before she retired she taught bible studies, had an administrative position and served her community as sacristan. She is currently involved with Amnesty International, and is a poet and writer.

LYDIA M COLLADO (1959–   ) Professed 1993 Filipino

Lydia has held ministries in the University of Manila and among the poor. She is currently preparing for her final profession with an international group in Rome. She is the youngest of our contributors, and based her contribution on the year she spent with the Duchesne Community in London.

JOAN FABER (1925–   ) Professed 1954 English

Joan spent her early ministry in schools and school administration. From 1970–5 she was responsible for the Society's international formation; this was followed by a period of provincial administration which she combined with training as a psychotherapist. She is now part of a community which has recently been established in a deprived area of London. She continues to work as a psychotherapist and is working with an AIDS project.

BARBARA HOGG (1901–1993) Professed 1939 English

Before the First World War Barbara spent two years in the Sacred Heart school in Liege, Belgium, where she received the seed of faith; there she met Reverend Mother Stuart. She was received into the Catholic Church as an adult and entered the Society two years later. Her active religious life was taken up with teaching, mainly mathematics, to the seniors. After 'retirement' she was actively engaged in the Society's formation. For the last twenty years of her life she worked on translations of Society texts. In 1989 both her legs were amputated, but she learnt to walk with artificial limbs and was frequently called upon by the Roehampton Limb Fitting Centre to demonstrate her skill.

PATRICIA MACKLE (1908–   ) Professed 1936 New Zealander

Patricia studied at the Universities of Sydney and Edinburgh and throughout her active life she has taught secondary and tertiary students. She has also held senior administrative posts. She is currently teaching English as a second language to South-East Asian students.

FRANCES MAKOWER (1930–   ) Professed 1976 British

Frances was brought up as a liberal Jew. She was received into the Roman Catholic Church as a young adult, but had to delay her entry to the noviceship for about ten years for health reasons. She taught for many years and worked for several years with homeless youngsters and drug users, until 1985 when she had to abandon active work. Since then she has lived at Duchesne House; she is a freelance journalist and writer.

REBECCA OGILVIE FORBES (1895–   ) Professed 1923 Scottish

'Becca was received into the Society by Reverend Mother Stuart. She spent the first part of her active ministry teaching; after a period of responsibility in school she was appointed to Society administration. She was an ex officio member of the Special Chapter in Rome, called in 1967. She retired the following year and was an active member of several communities before she came to Duchesne House, where she has lived since 1986.

APRIL O'LEARY (1922–   ) Professed 1955 British

April taught secondary and tertiary pupils until her retirement from teaching in 1978. Since then she has been a member of the team responsible for the House of Prayer in Brecon, Wales and the Spirituality Centre at Woldingham, where she has continued her work with retreatants and those seeking spiritual guidance. She wrote *Living Tradition*, a history of the Roehampton/Woldingham School, which was published in 1992.

PALMIRA DE OROVIO (1901–92) Professed 1929 Spanish

Palmira spent her active life as an educator in secondary schools where she also held senior administrative posts. In later life she became an active and enthusiastic member of the charismatic movement. She had literary gifts and wrote both prose and verse in celebration of feasts and community events.

CLARE SHANLEY (1904–   ) Professed 1946 British

Clare has spent most of her active life in school, both as a teacher and in administration. She retired from school work in 1971, but maintains many contacts with past pupils. Her hobbies include dressmaking and toy making – especially bears.

CARMEN SMITH (1920–   ) Professed 1949 American

Carmen has taught literature and religion during her active religious life; she has contributed regularly to the *American RSCJ Reflection Journal* and is a member of the Journal's editorial board. She retired in 1991 and moved from Grand Coteau to the novitiate in Cambridge, Boston. She is currently working as a volunteer in a local hospice.

ARATI (KATHLEEN) SNOW (1903–1988) Professed 1947 English

Arati spent much of her early life in the Middle East and was drawn from an early age to the world of Islam. She was an Anglican and developed a strong missionary vocation which led her to enter with the Anglican Sisters of the Epiphany of Calcutta, whom she left shortly before her proposed final profession in order to become a Catholic. In due course she entered the Irish province of the Society and was sent to India immediately after her profession. At first she taught, but spent the last twenty years before her death at the Christa Prema Seva Ashram in Pune. She was a fluent linguist and her deep, scholarly and sympathetic understanding of Islam was widely appreciated.

MARGARET TOURNOUR (1921–   ) Professed 1960 English

Margaret studied at Croydon School of Art and worked for the Oxford University Press as a children's book illustrator. She was an Anglican who was received into the Roman Catholic Church and later entered the Society. For most of her active life as a religious she taught young children; since retirement she has returned to book illustrating.

BRIGITTE TRIBOT LASPIÈRE (1925–   ) Professed 1956 French

Brigitte taught in the Society's schools, and served in its formation work both in France, Zaire and Rome, where she was responsible for the international formation programme. She has spent much of her active life in Africa and is currently in Chad where she is teaching and running catechetical programmes.

MARGARET WILLIAMS (1902–   ) Professed 1933 American

Margret has been a teacher of literature all her active religious life. When she retired from teaching she moved from New York to Kenwood, Albany, where she continues her research on the history of the Society of the Sacred Heart. Much of her work has been published, including her well-known biography of the founder of the Society of the Sacred Heart, *Saint Madeleine Sophie: Her Life and Letters.*

PRUE WILSON (1921–   ) Professed 1951 Scottish

Prue spent her active religious life in secondary and tertiary education and in provincial administration. She has recently returned from Uganda where she served for several years; she is currently teaching part time. In 1984 Darton, Longman and Todd published her book, *My Father Took Me to the Circus: Religious Life from Within.*